W9-AUZ-326

WRESTLING SUPERST★RS

UNDERTAKER

BY RAY McCLELLAN

EPIC

BELLWETHER MEDIA • MINNEAPOLIS, MN

EPIC BOOKS are no ordinary books. They burst with intense action, high-speed heroics, and shadows of the unknown. Are you ready for an Epic adventure?

This edition first published in 2015 by Bellwether Media, Inc.

No part of this publication may be reproduced in whole or in part without written permission of the publisher. For information regarding permission, write to Bellwether Media, Inc., Attention: Permissions Department, 5357 Penn Avenue South, Minneapolis, MN 55419.

Library of Congress Cataloging-in-Publication Data

McClellan, Ray.
 Undertaker / by Ray McClellan.
     pages cm. – (Epic: Wrestling Superstars)
 Includes bibliographical references and index.
 Summary: "Engaging images accompany information about Undertaker. The combination of high-interest subject matter and light text is intended for students in grades 2 through 7"– Provided by publisher.
 ISBN 978-1-62617-147-3 (hardcover : alk. paper)
 1. Undertaker, 1965–Juvenile literature. 2. Wrestlers–United States–Biography–Juvenile literature. I. Title.
 GV1196.U54M33 2014
 796.812092–dc23
 [B]
                              2014009104

Printed in the United States of America, North Mankato, MN.

TABLE OF CONTENTS

WARNING!

The wrestling moves used in this book are performed by professionals.
Do not attempt to reenact any of the moves performed in this book.

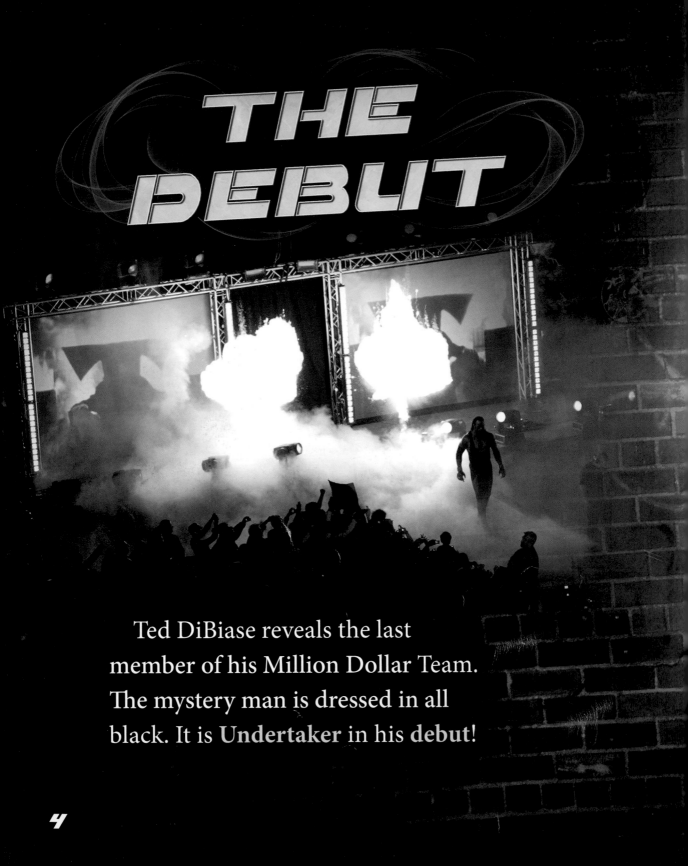

THE DEBUT

Ted DiBiase reveals the last member of his Million Dollar Team. The mystery man is dressed in all black. It is **Undertaker** in his **debut**!

Undertaker stares down the Dream Team. Soon he crushes Koko B. Ware with his Tombstone Piledriver. Then he **pins** Dusty Rhodes. Only a **countout** removes the new **Phenom**.

KOKO B. WARE

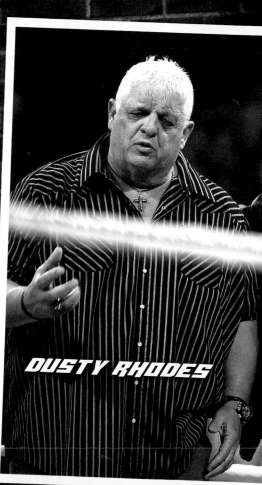

DUSTY RHODES

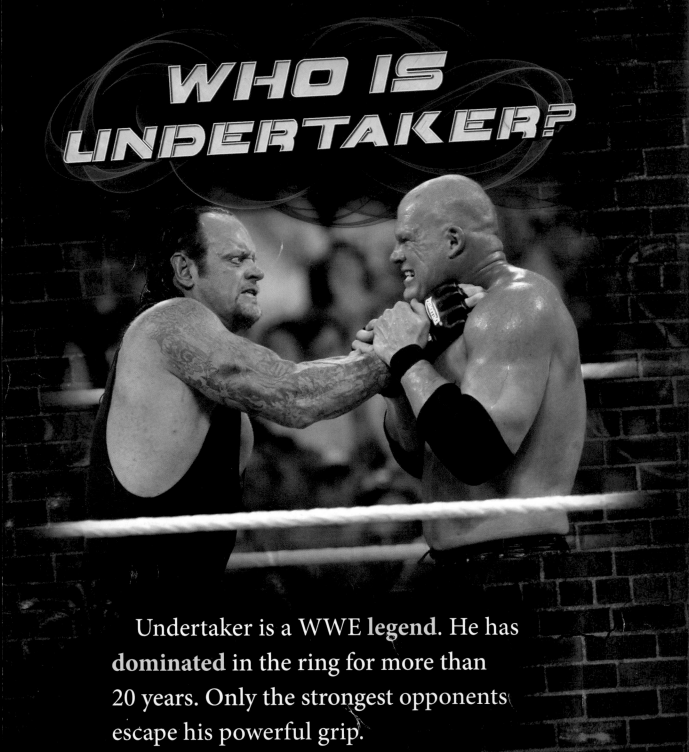

WHO IS UNDERTAKER?

Undertaker is a WWE **legend**. He has **dominated** in the ring for more than 20 years. Only the strongest opponents escape his powerful grip.

DONE FOR

Early on, Undertaker stuffed
opponents into body bags.
This is how he carried losers
out of the ring.

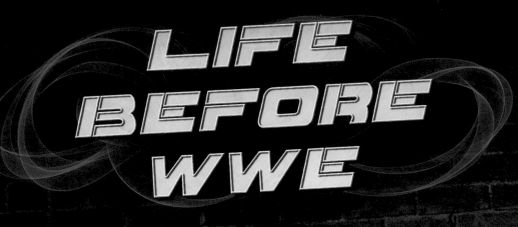

LIFE BEFORE WWE

In high school and college,
Undertaker was a basketball star.
His coaches knew he had talent.
They thought he could go pro.

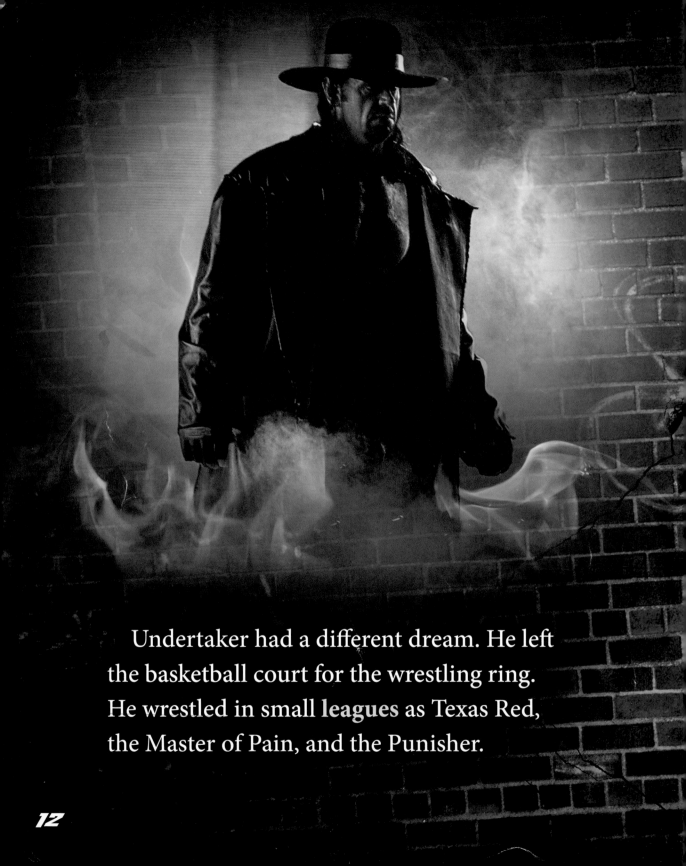

Undertaker had a different dream. He left the basketball court for the wrestling ring. He wrestled in small **leagues** as Texas Red, the Master of Pain, and the Punisher.

A WWE SUPERSTAR

STAR PROFILE

WRESTLING NAME: Undertaker

REAL NAME: Mark William Calaway

BIRTHDATE: March 24, 1965

HOMETOWN: Houston, Texas

HEIGHT: 6 feet, 10 inches (2.1 meters)

WEIGHT: 299 pounds (136 kilograms)

WWE DEBUT: 1990

FINISHING MOVE: Tombstone Piledriver

In 1990, Undertaker joined WWE as a **heel**. He appeared to feel no pain. Fans soon expected him to **no-sell** in his matches.

Over the years, Undertaker has changed looks and **tag team partners**. However, he has remained a champion. He won matches at WrestleMania for 21 years in a row.

EVIL EYES

★

Undertaker is known to roll his eyes back into his head. This scares his opponents.

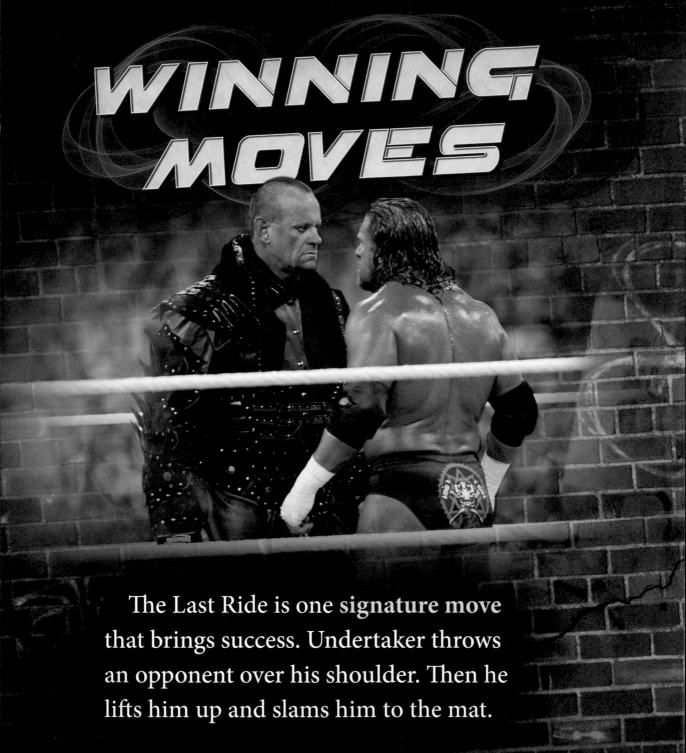

WINNING MOVES

The Last Ride is one **signature move** that brings success. Undertaker throws an opponent over his shoulder. Then he lifts him up and slams him to the mat.

THE
LAST RIDE

19

TOMBSTONE
PILEDRIVER

The Tombstone Piledriver is Undertaker's famous **finishing** move. He holds an opponent upside down. Then he falls to his knees. This pounds the opponent's head into the mat. BAM!

RIP

A "Rest in Peace" pin often follows this finisher. The hold positions the opponent like a dead body in a coffin.

GLOSSARY

countout—when a wrestler is out of the ring for longer than it takes to count to ten; a countout is an elimination.

debut—first official appearance

dominated—controlled with the use of power

finishing move—a wrestling move that finishes off an opponent

heel—a wrestler viewed as a villain

leagues—groups of people or teams united by a common activity

legend—a star who has lasting fame

no-sell—to show no reaction to an opponent's moves

phenom—an extremely talented person who shows great potential

pins—holds a wrestler down on the mat to end a match

signature move—a move that a wrestler is famous for performing

tag team partners—wrestlers who are teammates in the ring

undertaker—a person who prepares dead bodies and plans funeral

TO LEARN MORE

At the Library

Black, Jake. *WWE General Manager's Handbook*. New York, N.Y.: Grosset & Dunlap, 2012.

McClellan, Ray. *Kane*. Minneapolis, Minn.: Bellwether Media, 2015.

West, Tracey. *Race to the Rumble*. New York, N.Y.: Grosset & Dunlap, 2011.

On the Web

Learning more about Undertaker is as easy as 1, 2, 3.

1. Go to www.factsurfer.com.

2. Enter "Undertaker" into the search box.

3. Click the "Surf" button and you will see a list of related web sites.

With factsurfer.com, finding more information is just a click away.